Let's Explore Frankenmuth

By Zachary Malott
with some help from daddy
©2011, MM Publishing

This book is dedicated to none other
than the really great people and businesses in Frankenmuth
Never have we felt so welcome in any other place in the world ! ! ! !
WE LOVE FRANKENMUTH !

ACKNOWLEDGEMENTS

Thanks to the Zehnder families, special thanks to Michael Zehnder, Don Keller and Al Zehnder who did so much to help us with this project. Thanks to all the nice people at City Hall, Charlie Graham, Jamie Furbush, Peggy Reinhardt, Frankenmuth Bavarian Inn, Mary and the wonderful people at the Frankenmuth Historic Museum, Jerry & the folks at Frankenmuth Fun Ships, Anita Stefanovsky, Jim Engel, the Bourdows & Ebenhoes, Jimmy & Kenny Mosner, Gary Feria, all the great folks at The Frankenmuth News, Frankenmuth Chamber of Commerce, Anmar Sarafa & Frankenmuth Brewery, Andreas Schwarzkopf, big thanks to Judy and The Frankenmuth Toy Co. always our first stop in F'Muth, also Thomas Sells and the folks at GG's Sweets & Treats, Gary and the folks at Charlin's Book Nook, Captain Mitch Quirin and he folks of the Bavarian Belle, Kevin Kern, Ed Seargent and the folks at Grandpa Tiny's Farm, Zak & the folks at Frankenmuth Fudge and all the great folks and businesses at River Place, Ken, Marie and the great people at Satow Drugs, Scott at the Mirror Maze, Lori Libka & all the Bronner's folks, Jon & Tracy at The Michigan Shoppe, Steve Jennings, Amber Barckholtz, and Lori and the folks at Bronner's and all the great people of Frankenmuth!

Zach's Lederhosen courtesy of Andreas Schwarzkopf/Bavarian Specialties

Contact Zachary at CAATalent@Hotmail.Com
See all the "Let's Explore" Book Series Titles At
www.ZachsCorporation.Com

Willkommen (which means welcome in German)

Frankenmuth is a very small charming town in Michigan that has more to offer than even some major cities. It is called "Michigan's Little Bavaria" because it is very rich in German heritage and culture. In fact, 53% of Frankenmuth's residents are of German decent. It is just like being in Germany when you come to visit Frankenmuth.

The founding of Frankenmuth can be attributed back to a German missionary whose name was Frederick Wyneken. He had spent time in Michigan, Ohio, and Indiana and in 1840, he wrote to friends back in Germany asking for their help. Many early German immigrants suffered hard times and there was no Lutheran pastors, churches, or schools.

One man back in Germany by the name of Wilhelm Loehe, took interest in his letter and the situation of the German pioneers. Mr. Loehe was a very influential man back in Germany and started to train both teachers and pastors to come over to the United States.

Loehe wrote a pastor who was already in Michigan about finding a spot to start the colony for the people who were departing from Germany to answer Wyneken's call for assistance. Loehe decided on a location along the Cass River and decided it would be called, Frankenmuth. In German "Franken" stands for the Province of Franconia in the Kingdom of Bavaria and the word "Muth" means courage. Hence Frankenmuth means "courage of the Franconians".

A group of thirteen people comprised mostly of farmers agreed to make the long and risky trip to America to start this colony. Loehe recruited a former German teacher from England's, Oxford University to be the colony's leader and pastor.

They all met several times to discuss and prepare for their journey during the 1844-45 winter season and established their constitution for the colony, which outlined their responsibilities to each other and the church. The colonists all pledged their loyalty to Germany and the German language.

Frankenmuth would be exclusively a German-Lutheran colony.

The group departed Nuernberg on the 5th of April, 1845 and traveled far on foot, wagons, and by train to reach Bremerhafen where their ship, "The Caroline" waited for them. Departing Bremerhafen headed for New York City, the ship and crew faced many challenges and hardship. Their ship ran aground on a sand bar on the Weser River. Because of storms, the ship was forced to sail around Scotland instead of through the English Channel. The journey across the Atlantic was strenuous, challenging violent storms, seasickness, a collision with another ship, shortage of food and even an outbreak of small pox which tragically claimed the life of one of the colonies children.

The ship and crew were driven far north and had to navigate through icebergs and thick fog for several days. Still their determination and courage proved strong and the ship finally reached New York Harbor on June 8, 1845 after spending more than a month and a half at sea.

The Caroline

From New York, the colonists started out for Michigan. They sailed on several steamboats to make the journey including a week-long trip by sailboat to arrive eventually in Bay City. The group then literally pulled the ship fifteen miles up the Saginaw River to reach Saginaw and there they established a temporary camp, while some from the group journeyed ahead in search of an exact location for the new colony to call home.

A young Frankenmuth community

On August 18, 1845, the colonists packed up their belongings into an oxcart and made the twelve mile walk through forests and swamps to finally arrive right here in Frankenmuth.

Each of the colony's members took their own 120 acre plot of farm land. The group had purchased a total of 680 acres of Indian Reservation land from the federal government.

In 1846, another group of emigrants from Germany left Germany for Frankenmuth. This group was considerably larger with approximately ninety members who followed the same path as the original settlers of 1845. Now the colony was growing in size, many were farmers and others would lead the way in the development of Frankenmuth's business community.

Early town of Frankenmuth

The town of Frankenmuth was built about a mile away from the location of the original settlement. In 1847, a dam and mill were built on the Cass River. Frankenmuth flourished from the production of flour, beer, cheese, sausage and for its saw and flour mills.

Some of these names, are still found today in Frankenmuth, the direct descendants of the original founding families of Frankenmuth.

The development of tourism in Frankenmuth can be mainly attributed to three primary people, brothers William & Edwin Zehnder and Wally Bronner. The present location of Zehnder's Restaurant originally housed the Exchange Hotel built by Henry Reichle back in 1856 and remained a hotel up until 1876. In 1927, the hotel was purchased by William Zehnder Sr. who remodeled the building to resemble Mount Vernon.

Frankenmuth is now home to just under 5000 people who live here. Frankenmuth is surrounded by farms and many of Frankenmuth's farms have been the home to generations of families. Frankenmuth people are very proud and take great pride in their community. People come from all over the world just to see this town.

Hi, my name is Zachary, and I'm going to take you on a tour through this fascinating town. Although there are many interesting things to see all over town, Main Street is where most of the excitement in Frankenmuth is situated. It is Frankenmuth's main business district.

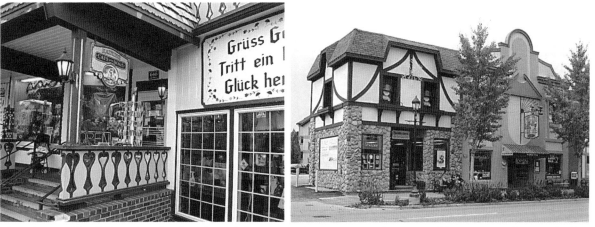

Bavarian themed buildings line both sides of the street, housing a wide array of businesses from gift shops to candy shops to toy shops. It is a very exciting place for young folks like us. I always have a whole day full of fun when we visit here.

Many buildings look like they came straight from an Alpine village. They have a very unique style. This is known as "Franconian-style" architecture.

There are so many unique shops throughout Main Street to explore.

From street side dining in an original turn of the century restaurant, or a cozy little coffee house.

To several places to see fudge and other candy made.

to the little country store.

The Frankenmuth Clock Company is a great place to see, especially on the hour!

To the very popular Frankenmuth Cheese Haus, which has an incredible selection of over 140 kinds of cheese.

Zehnder's opened in 1929, and has been serving chicken dinners since.

Zehnder's famous neon sign, erected in 1936 is the longest continually used neon sign in existence.

Zehnder's is the largest family restaurant in America.

The world famous Zehnder's Restaurant is situated on the former site of the New Exchange Hotel, the first restaurant meals in Frankenmuth were served here on this spot. Zehnder's has a total of nine dining rooms and can serve up to 1500 guests at one time. The location also houses a bakery, food store, and a gift shop. My daddy worked here one summer when he was in high school.

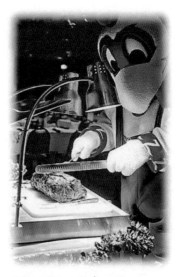

Meet Drumstick, Zehnder's official mascot.

The Frankenmuth Bavarian Inn has been a Frankenmuth landmark since 1888. The restaurant is renowned for its world famous family style chicken dinners and since opening they have served over 20 Million of them. However, their menu is full of great German dishes with funny German names like; Schnitzel, Sauerbraten, and Wiener Schnitzel. They have a total of 12 dining rooms which are all themed like Olde World Germany.

Their chicken dinners are truly "world famous".

The building housed the Fischer's Hotel for many years up until 1950, when the building was purchased by the Zehnder brothers.

The building was remodeled to its present Bavarian theme in 1955, after the brothers returned from a vacation in Bavaria.

The Bavarian Inn building is like a village of its own, with many dining rooms and a whole basement full of little shops including a toy store.

The Bavarian Inn's Glockenspiel

Is a 35 bell carillon that was imported from Germany in October 1967. In English, Glockenspiel means "bells play".

The bells play at noon, 3PM, 6PM, and 9PM every day and can be heard for miles.

The tower features figures that were carved from wood from the Black Forrest and run on four tracks depicting the story of the Pied Piper of Hameln.

The Glockenspiel is one of Frankenmuth's must see attractions and is really neat!

The Bavarian Inn's, Covered Bridge & Leather Gift Shop is on the opposite end of the parking lot and worth a visit.

Zehnder's Holz Brucke (wooden bridge)

Is a three span town lattice covered bridge is 239 feet and spans the Cass River. It is constructed mainly of Douglas Fir and features two lanes of traffic for cars and pedestrian walkways on each side. It joins the town with the Bavarian Inn's hotel and Frankenmuth's fair grounds and park.

The bridge was the brainchild of Eddie and William "Tiny" Zehnder and was built by Milton S Graton, who spent two years constructing the bridge. Two oxen pulled the bridge into place using a block-capstan pulley system. The process took a total of twelve days to get the bridge positioned into place.

Wooden pegs are used to hold the pieces of wood together, the same fashion as they were hundreds of years ago.

The bridge was completed on January 29, 1980 and dedicated September 9, 1980.

ALL ABOARD! The Bavarian Belle, Frankenmuth's own full-size authentic paddlewheel river boat. They give a great narrated tour of Frankenmuth on the Cass River.

Passengers will enjoy a relaxing and scenic journey along the Cass River.

The Bavarian Belle is docked at the River Place and make sure you ask about her incredible journey she went through to reach her Frankenmuth home.

Horse drawn carriages are a popular way to explore the sights of Frankenmuth.

Frankenmuth's carriages are similar to the luxury afforded to royalty and the prices to ride are pretty reasonable.

The best place to catch a carriage is down by Zehnder's and the Bavarian Inn.

Funships offer 12 passenger electric boats that take passengers on a relaxing and informative cruise along the Cass River.

A popular special River Cruise features the guests being served with chocolate that is handmade in the FunShips very own store!

Funships also rents things called, "Aqua Cycles" for those who want to do it themselves using pedal power instead.

Frankenmuth River Place is another must see for visitors!

There is so much to see and do at River Place, plan on spending some time here.

River Place is an outdoor mall featuring over forty unique shops and some spectacular architecture. It is located next to the Bavarian Inn, and you can cross over the Cass River on the pedestrian bridge which has a great view of the covered bridge. Many exciting events are held here annually including a clam & lobster festival, a scarecrow fest, a holiday candlewalk, a dog bowl, and even a pet adopt-a-thon.

River Place is like its very own little village, full of colorful Franconian style buildings.

and very interesting shops...

One store that you don't want to miss is, Our Mother Earth. The store is decorated like a jungle and has all kinds of really neat and unique things. They have a huge selection of stuffed animals.

Here Comes Treble, has everything you could think of relating to music and well known music groups.

This is my daddy's favorite store without question. Last time we were in town, daddy bought a leopard tie, so you see they have all kinds of stuff to see and buy and most are things you won't find anywhere else or didn't think even existed.

The Michigan Shoppe is full of Michigan themed items, including gifts, foods, and souvenirs.

Every Michigan thing you could possibly think of is in here!

Hello Cats & Dogs, is the place to find anything you could ever imagine for your pet.

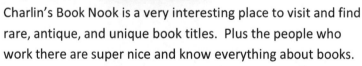

Charlin's Book Nook is a very interesting place to visit and find rare, antique, and unique book titles. Plus the people who work there are super nice and know everything about books.

The Bead Haven, has over a million beads under their roof, plus free classes to learn how to make stuff.

24

Several candy makers are located in The River Place.

Don't miss Peace Frogs for everything frog related!

How about a maze made of mirrors for fun? It's not as easy as you think, but lots of fun!

Humor Us, is a really, really fun store and has all kinds of super neat and unusual stuff. If you like nostalgic stuff, they have lots of that too.

The River Place has a really neat miniature version of Frankenmuth's famous covered bridge. In fact, their landscape and architecture throughout is nothing less than impressive.

Everything is here, from an awesome arcade to Play games…….

…..to a old fashion stagecoach

Not to mention the spectacular views of the bridge and waterfall you get from The River Place.

The Frankenmuth Toy Company and Kite Kraft on Main Street is a great big toy store and kite shop and one of my first and favorite stops. I love Playmobil toys and they have one of the biggest selections I've seen. In fact, they have so many toys to look at that you should plan on spending some time here.

Frankenmuth has several great toy stores.

There are also the toy stores in the basement of the Bavarian Inn and River Place.

Rau's Country Store has been a Frankenmuth tradition for decades and what country store would be without the old fashion pickle jar? But it doesn't stop there. Rau's has been in operation for three generations and carries a stock of over 40,000 unique items. Rau's features three floors full of everything from dry goods, neat things for the house to miniature doll houses and a huge supply of doll house stuff, toys, metal signs, lots of old nostalgic items and just everything under the sun.

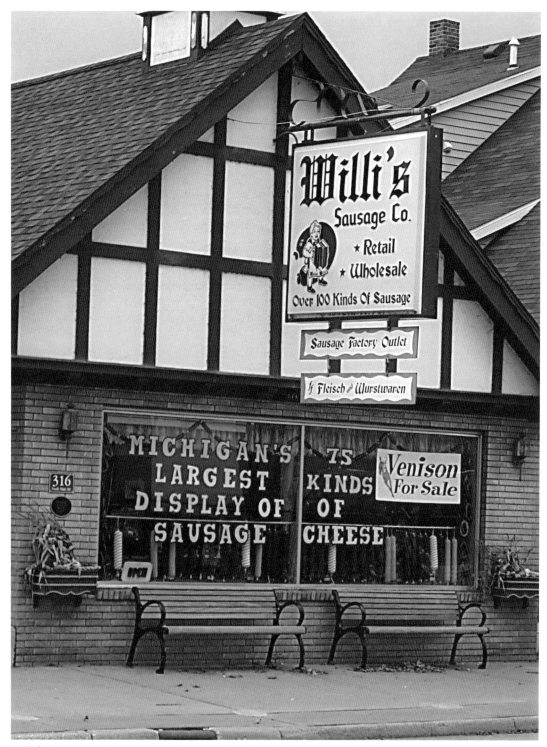

Willi's Sausage Company is located on Main Street and is home to over 100 different types of meat including Ostrich and Buffalo. Willi's makes all their own sausages and jerky, and brats and stuff and also features a selection of over 75 different types of cheese.

Charlie & Matt Kern cooking bratwurst outside Of Kern's Sausage back In 1958.

Today the Kern family tradition continues.

Kern's Sausages opened for business in August of 1949, after Kern's founder, Marcus Kern, a lifetime resident of Frankenmuth was told by his doctor that he needed to find a new career that would allow him to work indoors. Kern purchased Charles Vanek's Corner Grocery and planned to open a modest mom & pop corner grocery and call it, Kern's Corner Grocery. Instead a dynasty for Frankenmuth's most famous sausages was born. The whole family worked in the store, Marcus's wife; Esther and the two sons, Charlie and Matt.

Kern's was in fact, the very first Frankenmuth business to use and promote the Bavarian theme. When Marcus passed away in 1969, the two sons took over and then in 1996, Charles Kern's two sons, Ron & Kevin took over the business, marking the third generation of Kern's to operate the family business.

The reputation Kern's carries for fine sausages and even cheeses continues today, offering over 34 different varieties of sausage.

Kern's is located on the south edge of town on Main Street.

Fischer Hall was built in the late 1800's and now hosts weddings, plays, concerts and other gatherings.

Fischer Hall is a popular location for local events and functions

The world's best root beer is made in Frankenmuth.

The Frankenmuth Brewery was founded in 1862 and it is the second oldest brewery in the United States.

This 28,000 square foot building houses two restaurants serving traditional American style dishes, and a huge outdoor dining area with their three huge patio's that overlook the Cass River.

The building also houses a micro-brewery and makes their very own "Frankie's Root Bier". Make sure you try it, it is the best!

The Frankenmuth Historical Museum is full of interesting things from Frankenmuth's long, rich, history.

The museum is housed in the former location of The Kern Commercial House Hotel, built in 1905. It once also housed the offices of the Frankenmuth News for several years.

Photo courtesy of Frankenmuth Historical Assoc.

Frankenmuth has some beautiful art. Above is the fountain in front of the Chamber of Commerce and Visitor's Center. To the right is a work of art next to the White House.

The Veteran's Memorial is on Main Street and has a beautiful garden.

The original Satow Drugs from 1937

Satow Drugs is an old fashioned drug store that has the old style soda fountain. Here you can relax in an almost 1950's style "soda shop" that they call Die Kaffee Stube. What's really special about this place is that my daddy used to eat here after school almost every day when Frankenmuth Middle School used to be across the street.

The Bavarian Inn Lodge is a spectacular resort that is just on the other side of the covered bridge. The place is so big that it has five indoor pools, an 18 hole indoor miniature golf course, two gift shops, game arcades, and on the grounds is a beautiful walking trail.

Not to forget about the pen with all the peacocks, roosters, and other birds.

Frankenmuth is home to the only repository in the United States to be centered around the wartime experiences of one state's veteran's.

Michigan's Own Military & Space Museum also houses the world's largest Medal of Honor collection.

The museum has a most impressive collection of artifacts, including items from all wars and even the space program.

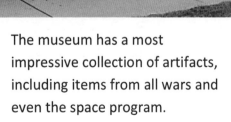

Grandpa Tiny's Farm is the result of a vision by William "Tiny" Zehnder of Frankenmuth Bavarian Inn fame. Mr. Zehnder had plans to build an authentic turn of the century working farm. The result is Grandpa Tiny's Farm, a place where visitors can see and get a hand's on experience with a real working farm.

The Barn

The farm house was built around the early 1900's and was moved to the farm in 1997. In 1999, a restoration committee started restoring the house.

Farm resident, "Tom the Turkey"

The Hart One Room Schoolhouse was built between 1855-1860, and was used for 70 years for students grades 1 to 8.

The "Weber Backofen" originated in Germany and is an outdoor oven, mostly used to bake bread.

There is much to see and do at Grandpa Tiny's, you can do all kinds of neat things.

Frankenmuth's famed "Black Bridge" is also at Grandpa Tiny's Farm and you have to cross it to get to the farm.

This bridge originally called the "Dehmel Road Bridge" was built in 1907 and is 151 feet in length. It is one of few "historic metal truss bridges"

William "Tiny" Zehnder had a love for historic bridges and literally had the bridge moved to the farm. Restoration on the bridge was completed in 2002.

The bridge which once crossed the Cass River now crosses Dead Creek.

Bronner's is probably the world's largest Christmas store and has everything related to the Christmas holidays.

It's Christmas year round at Bronner's, who are open 361 days a year.

Wally Bronner, founder of Bronner's Christmas Wonderland, played a significant part in the development of tourism for Frankenmuth.

Bronner's is known worldwide and people travel from far away to visit this magical Christmas wonderland.

Zehnder's Splash Village Hotel & Waterpark opened in 2005 and is a resort with its own 30,000 sq. foot indoor waterpark, complete with water tube slides, Crooked Brook Creek (an indoor lazy river) and huge play structures.

The Giggling Gorge and Perilous Plunge are both four stories high. The waterpark is open year round and daily and yearly passes are available to local residents, as well as, those staying at other nearby hotels or campsites.

They even offer swim lessons, and Splash Village has its very own gift shop, arcade and even a restaurant.

Imagine rushing four stories down a waterslide or floating along an indoor river!

Frankenmuth hosts a large parade down Main Street as one of the Highlights of the Bavarian Festival.

The Bavarian Festival is a major event that takes place each year in June.

The first Bavarian Fest took place way back in 1959. It is also rated as one of Michigan's top 5 festivals and attracts more than 10,000 visitors each year.

Zehnders SnowFest is an annual event that features
Incredible ice & snow carvings and much more.

A great fireworks show
closes out SnowFest.

Courtesy- MLive

Frankenmuth also has a great annual auto show and also an annual fire truck show.

44

So you see there is so much to see and do in Frankenmuth. It's a really great place to go for a weekend trip. Frankenmuth is even quite popular in the winter with visitors.

During the winter, Frankenmuth is even more stunningly beautiful

The old Lager Mill is an old millhouse on the river down by Zehnder's

Even on the outskirts of town, there is so much to see and do, including the Wilderness Trails Zoo.

EIN PROSIT DER GEMÜTLICHKEIT
(A Toast to Bavarian Hospitality)

The "Let's Explore" Book Series
www.zachscorporation.com